Text and illustration copyright © 2018, 2020 by Chris Ferrie

Cover and internal design © 2020 by Sourcebooks

Cover and internal design by Will Riley

Sourcebooks and the colophon are registered trademarks of Sourcebooks.

All rights reserved.

Published by Sourcebooks eXplore, an imprint of Sourcebooks Kids

P.O. Box 4410, Naperville, Illinois 60567–4410

(630) 961-3900

sourcebookskids.com

First published as Red Kangaroo's Thousands Physics Whys: *A Messy Room: Statistical Physics*

in 2018 in China by China Children's Press and Publication Group.

Library of Congress Cataloging-in-Publication Data is on file with the publisher.

Source of Production: PrintPlus Limited, Shenzhen, Guangdong Province, China

Date of Production: April 2020

Run Number: 5018390

Printed and bound in China.

PP 10 9 8 7 6 5 4 3 2 1

Let's Clean Up!

Unpacking the Science of Messy Rooms with Statistical Physics

#1 Bestselling
Science Author for Kids
Chris Ferrie

sourcebooks
eXplore

Red Kangaroo really needs to clean up her room.

"I wonder why it is so hard to keep my room clean," she says. "It always gets messy so quickly!"

She decides to go see Dr. Chris and ask for his help.

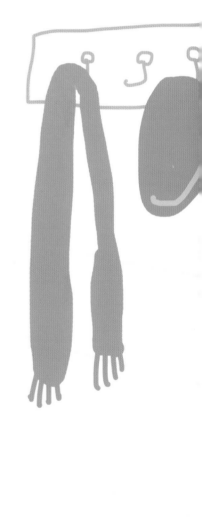

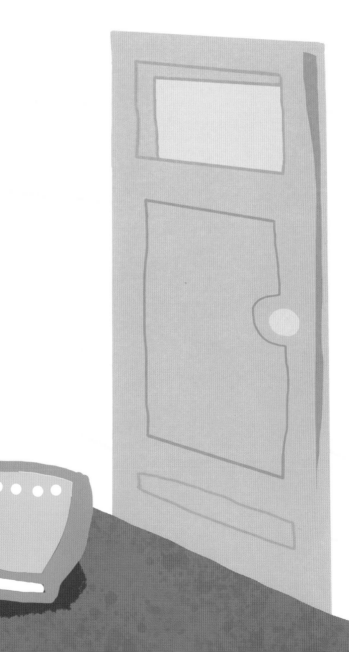

"Can you tell me why my room always gets so messy?" Red Kangaroo asks Dr. Chris.

"Of course!" he replies. "All you need to know is statistical physics. And if you can count, then it'll be easy to understand!"

"I can count!" Red Kangaroo says. "It's as easy as 1, 2, 3!"

"Counting will help you understand two ideas in physics," says Dr. Chris. "These ideas help explain a lot of things in the world. They explain why spilled water can't go back into a cup. Or why cooked food can't become uncooked. Or why you can't make a cracked egg become whole again."

"Wow! Physics can explain a lot of things!" Red Kangaroo says. "But none of that sounds like counting, Dr. Chris!"

"Let's start with a clean room and I'll explain," Dr. Chris says. "Your room is clean when everything is put away in the right place. That means there is only one way to have a clean room."

"If anything from your shelf is out of place, then your room is messy," Dr. Chris continues. "If you take one thing from the shelf, then you have four ways that your room can be messy."

Dr. Chris

"But what if more than one thing from the shelf is out of place?" Red Kangaroo asks.

"Great question!" says Dr. Chris. "If two things on your shelf are out of place, then you have even more ways to get a messy room. Can you count all the ways two things can be out of place?"

Dr. Chris

"Now let's take three things off the shelf," Dr. Chris says.

"That's easy to count," says Red Kangaroo. "If three things are on the floor, then only one thing is left on the shelf. That means there are four ways for three things to be out of place!"

Dr. Chris

"Can you count how many ways your room can be messy if you take everything off the shelf?" Dr. Chris asks.

"There's only one way for everything to be out of place!" says Red Kangaroo.

"Exactly!" Dr. Chris replies. "What a mess!"

"Now let's count all the ways your room can be messy," Dr. Chris says. "There are four ways one thing can be out of place, six ways two things can be out of place, four ways three things can be out of place, and one way everything can be out of place. Can you count the total number of ways your room can be messy?"

"No wonder it feels impossible to keep my room clean!" says Red Kangaroo. "There are fifteen ways my room can get messy and only one way for everything to be clean!"

"Now you understand the first idea I wanted to teach you," Dr. Chris says. "You just learned about **entropy.**"

"What-opy?" asks Red Kangaroo.

"Entropy means the number of ways something can look," says Dr. Chris. "A clean room has low entropy because there is only one way for it to be clean."

"I see! So my messy room has high entropy because there are fifteen ways for me to make a mess!" says Red Kangaroo.

"Great job!" Dr. Chris says. "You just learned the **Second Law of Thermodynamics**! This law says that all things increase in entropy. A whole egg, a glass of water, and raw food all have low entropy."

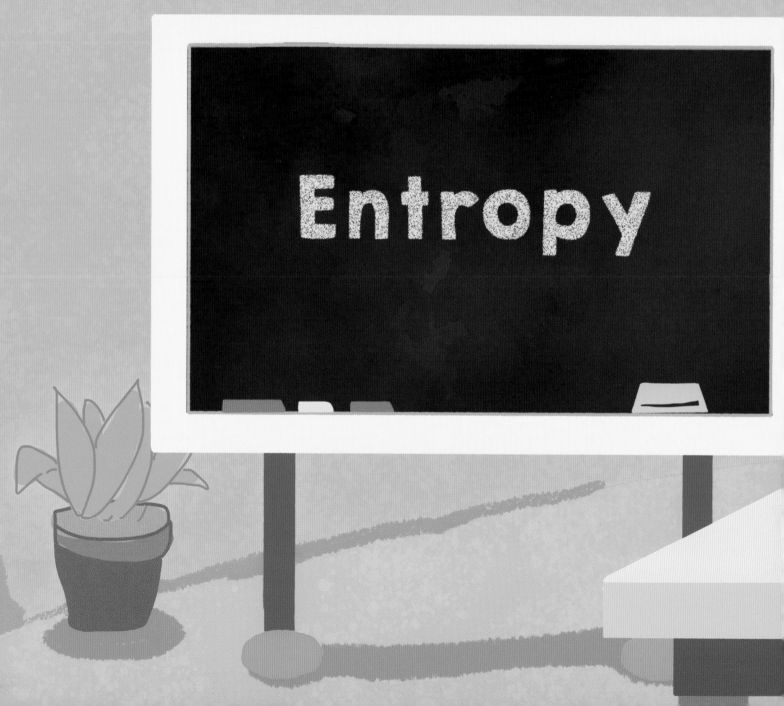

"But there are many ways to crack an egg and many ways to spill water and many ways to cook raw food!" says Red Kangaroo. "That's all high entropy!"

"Good job, Red Kangaroo!" says Dr. Chris. "Entropy increases all by itself. It would take a lot of work to try to decrease it."

"I've almost got my room all clean now, Dr. Chris!" Red Kangaroo says. "I am going to try and keep it that way!"

"You can try," says Dr. Chris. "But remember you have to work very hard against statistical physics!"

"I can do it!" says Red Kangaroo.

Glossary

Second Law of Thermodynamics

A law of physics that states everything naturally increases in entropy. It would take a lot of work or energy to decrease entropy.

Entropy

The number of ways specific details can change to create the same situation. Something can have either low entropy or high entropy.

Statistics

The science of counting, collecting, and reporting data.

Statistical Physics

The combination of statistics and physics to study why things made of lots of smaller things act the way they do.

Thermodynamics
A science of how energy transfers between two or more things.

Physics
The study of how matter and energy interact.

Show What You Know

1. List two situations that have low entropy.

2. List two situations that have high entropy.

3. Explain what the Second Law of Thermodynamics teaches us about how the world works.

4. True or False: You can decrease the entropy of something without effort.

5. Find an example (either from the book or in real life) where something goes from high entropy to low entropy.

Answers on the last page.

Test It Out

Shake it up!

1. You'll need a cardboard box (you could use a shoebox, pizza box, etc.), some extra cardboard, scissors, tape, and at least six marbles. If you don't have marbles, you can use any small objects that would easily move around inside the box.

2. Cut your extra cardboard to fit snugly inside the box, dividing it into two sides. Before you tape it down, cut an opening in the divider about twice the size of the marbles.

3. Slide the divider into the center of the box and use the tape to hold the divider in place.

4. Place all the marbles on one side of the box. Close the box and then shake it.

5. Make a prediction about where the marbles will be when you reopen the box.

6. Open it up and record your observation.

7. Statistical physics is about data (numbers). Try the experiment many times to see if the marbles end up in the same spot each time. Keep a record of what happens each time.

Count the number of times each situation happens. From these numbers, can you determine which situation has the lowest entropy? What about which situation has the highest entropy?

Mix it up!

1. You'll need three clear glasses of water, food coloring, and a timer.

2. You are going to drop food coloring into the water of each glass, but first make a prediction about what you think will happen after one minute. How will the food coloring spread in the water? Will all three glasses look the same? Now make a prediction of what will happen after ten minutes.

3. As quickly as possible (or with the help of multiple hands), put a single drop of food coloring in each glass. Start the timer.

4. After one minute, make your first observation. Has the food coloring spread? Does the pattern of color match your prediction? Does it look the same for every glass?

5. After ten minutes, make your second observation. Does it match your prediction?

Now answer this: Did the entropy of putting color in water increase or decrease over time?

What to expect when you Test It Out

Shake it up!

Every time you shake the box, the marbles will move in a different way. There is no way to predict where each will end up, but most likely you will have two or three marbles on each side of the box. Very rarely will you end up with only one or zero marbles on one side of the box. Like the clean room, there is only one way for the box to have all the marbles in their starting position. It must have low entropy.

Mix it up!

After one minute, the food coloring would have spread in the water. However, the pattern of color will probably look different in every glass. After ten minutes, the color would have spread more. The patterns most likely will still be different. Imagine the food coloring as small marbles starting in the same place and bouncing around. There is only one way for them to be in the same place, but there are so many ways for them to be spread out in the glass that you could never count them all!

Show What You Know answers

1. Answers will vary. Some examples: frozen water has lower entropy than liquid water; a clean room has lower entropy than a messy room; a piece of notebook paper has lower entropy than a shredded piece of paper.

2. Answers will vary. Some examples: boiling water has higher entropy than cool water; a broken egg has higher entropy than a whole egg; a baked cake has higher entropy than its separate ingredients.